The Fantasy Art of

MW00330844

The
Fantasy
Art of

**Oliver
Frey**

Roger Kean

THALAMUS

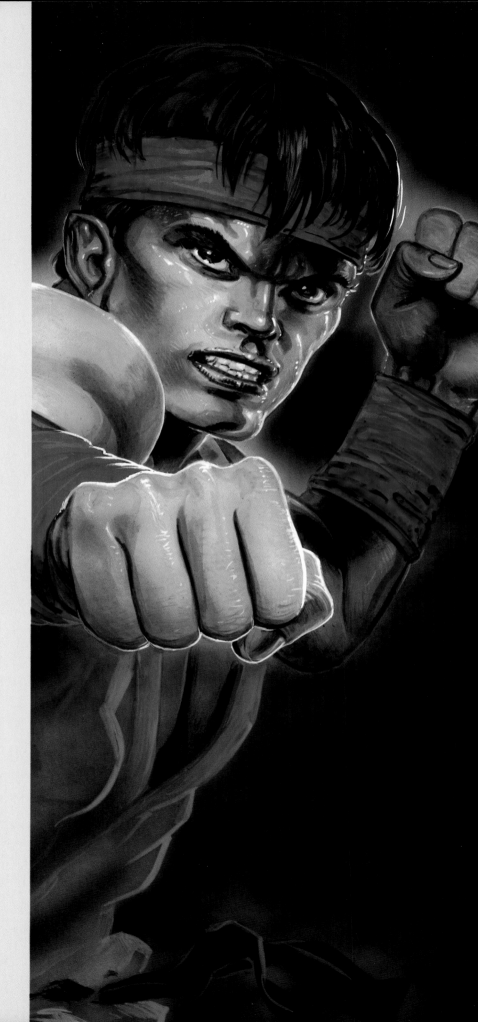

Thalamus Publishing is an imprint of
International Media Solutions Limited
4 Attorney's Walk, Bull Ring,
Ludlow, Shropshire SY8 1AA
England
Tel: +44 (0)1584 874977
Fax: +44 (0)1584 872125
www.thalamus-books.com

© 2006 Thalamus Publishing
Design © Thalamus Publishing 2006

The rights of Roger Kean to be identified as the Author of
this Work has been asserted by him in accordance with the
Copyright, Designs and Patents Act 1988. All rights
reserved.

No part of this book may be reproduced or utilised in any
form or by any means, electronic or mechanical, including
photocopying, recording or by any information storage or
retrieval systems, without permission in writing from the
publisher.

British Library Cataloguing in Publication Data
A CIP Data Record for this book
is available from the British Library
ISBN 1-902886-06-2

Typeset in Fairfield and Helvetica Neue Condensed

Printed and bound in Singapore
This book is printed on acid-free paper

10 9 8 7 6 5 4 3 2 1

Acknowledgements

For their support, advice and constructive criticism,
many thanks to Rob de Voogd (Mr. Zzapback),
Craig Grannell (CoverCritic) and Stephen Stuttard
(Mr. ScanMania); and – well, for just being there –
the two primary web sites – Matthew Wilson's Crash
Online (www.crashonline.org.uk) and Iain Black's
The DEF Guide to ZZAP!64 (www.zzap64.co.uk).

Thanks to Stephen Stuttard for providing so many of
the magazine cover scans (excepting *Fear* and
Frighteners) and for remembering many forgotten
masterpieces, and Rob de Voogd for the 'New
Zealand' scan from *Look & Learn* on page 21 and
permission to use quotations from the DEF Tribute to
Zzap!64 on page 38.

All pictures © Oliver Frey, except: 6, 11 top left,
20 bottom right, 29 bottom right, 30 (Roger Kean);
13 comparison art from Don Lawrence and
Frank Bellamy; 37 top (Matthew Uffindell);
20 top (photograph by Don Green, in the author's
possession).

Detail from the cover of
the TOPPS/Merlin sticker
album of Capcom's
Street Fighter II. 1992

CONTENTS

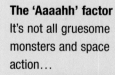

The 'Aaaahh' factor
It's not all gruesome monsters and space action…

FOREWORD

Oliver Frey is uncomfortable with being referred to as an 'artist'. He calls himself a 'commercial illustrator'; yet despite the modesty of the term he has entertained and often inspired generations with his unique vision of the world. His prolific output is definitely of a fantastic nature although the imagery is almost always bound to a sense of reality.

My involvement with Oliver has been a long and rewarding one, and continues to be so. I first met him in January 1969 when we were both starting a two-year course at the London Film School, and we have worked together in one capacity or another ever since. In the cavernous, dusty warehouse on Sheldon Street, just off Long Acre in Covent Garden, that housed the school in those days, many friendships were forged; but I never then anticipated the privilege of being associated with one of Britain's best action illustrators. In fact, on that first day of orientation, strapped tightly into a blue-grey, somewhat military looking raincoat, my first impression was of a 'typically' uptight Germanic-Swiss student of deadly serious demeanour. I only discovered a few weeks later that his mother-tongue was Italian, and that Oliver had inherited a Mediterranean character that often led to explosive arguments – especially if anyone maligned his favourite movie heroes, James Bond and the 'Man With No Name'.

Since I have been a witness to and a participant in many of the events described in this book, it is inevitable that my presence hovers above the text. However, I am uncomfortable at mentioning myself in the first person because I feel it intrudes on the narrative, and for this reason on the occasions my presence crops up, I have referred to myself in the third person.

A few of Oliver's quotations in the following piece have been taken from an interview with him published in issue 24 of *CRASH* magazine (Christmas 1985). Others have come in part from several other interviews conducted wth him over the years, and many culled from the man directly (which is hard work, since he holds many opinions on almost everything, except himself). The commentaries on the pictures are Oliver's own words, although sometimes with my own additions where it helps illuminate aspects of his art that he fails to see himself.

Over the years, Oliver Frey has gained a huge and appreciative fan base – which knows him familiarly as 'Oli' – and yet, because he is first and foremost a commercial artist, much of his most exciting work, especially for magazine covers, has been designed for and defaced by the blather of 'cover lines' selling the contents. Few people will ever have seen the unadulterated originals without them; surely the only excuse needed for this book?   **Roger Kean**

Notes on the text:

When given, dimensions (*width x height*) are of original, not reproduced size. All paintings are in inks, acrylics or a combination on artboard, unless otherwise stated. Dates given are generally for the time of painting, not of publication.

Portrait of Oliver Frey at Highgate, 1974.

Oil on hardboard, Roger Kean

The launch of Crash Micro Games Action, 1983.
Clockwise from the top left: Oliver's brother Franco, Roger Kean and Oliver Frey pose in terrible peril.

'We created two publicity shots to be printed in the computer games magazines, and as part of a local PR campaign [the other can be seen on page 9]. This one was photographed in my dining room in Ludlow on my studio Minolta camera, using the auto-timer to get all three of us in the shot. For lighting, we had several movie studio lights I had owned for years. The prints were enlarged to "ten-by-twelves" on a matt paper, and then I airbrushed and painted in the monster and other details with Indian ink and one called "bleed-white".'

A BOOM IN VIDEOGAMES, LUDLOW 1983

Early in 1983, Oliver Frey's younger brother Franco visited him at his Shropshire home in Ludlow and showed him a new toy. It was a Sinclair ZX81 'home' computer – and amazingly it played games in glorious black and white. Frey the elder was clearly unimpressed, but Franco persisted and a month later reappeared with an even bigger and better machine, a 16K Sinclair Spectrum – and that boasted colour.

Franco had discovered that few shops stocked the games for this new youth fad, and enthusiastically proposed starting a mail order firm to satisfy the growing demand for Spectrum software. And so a partnership was formed between Franco, Oliver and Roger Kean, which they called Crash Micro Games Action. People in the business were bemused by the use of the word 'Crash' – hardly a positive term in computer-speak, but Oliver, who suggested it, liked its aggressive quality; short, sharp and to the point.

The phenomenon that eventually became *CRASH* magazine was almost stillborn. The partnership only had £2,500 in funds, raised by Kean on a credit card loan – ostensibly for a new kitchen. Most of that vanished in the cost of advertising in the fledgling computer games magazines and in purchasing advance stock. The first mail order advertisement appeared in *Personal Computer Games* in July 1983, and then others followed in *Computer & Video Games*, *Sinclair User* and *Popular Computing Weekly*.

Oliver had strong ideas of how these half- and quarter-pages should look to make them stand out. They were comprised of a long list of titles with a tick box for each. Logically, such a crowded space should be black text on a white background, but he threw all traditional

Roger Kean, Frano Frey and Oliver Frey pose in the second of the PR photographs, taken in Ludlow during 1983. It featured Franco's super smooth Pontiac Transam in the town's famous Broad Street. Even today, some Ludlow inhabitants swear they remember the UFOs sailing overhead, thanks to Oliver's painted additions to the print.

Below: An example of Crash Micro Games Action's reversed out magazine ads for mail order, and two pages from one of the illustrated catalogues.

wisdom to the wind and reversed everything out. The result turned a potentially boring advertisement into something eye-catching. And it worked. The first trickle of orders turned into a flood, the mailing list of names grew and Crash Micro Games Action launched the main thrust of its business. This was a cheaply produced mail order catalogue, with short reviews of the product to entice customers to buy more.

Oliver's illustrative skills were the secret weapon. Mailings of the time were generally uninspiring list of titles, but Crash Micro Games Action catalogues were enlivened by drawings. These were pure interpretations of what the blobs, squiggles and dots of an early Spectrum game were supposed to look like in a gameplayer's mind. Any spare half-inch around the margins and between the columns was also filled in with a variety of small creatures, and the famous 'Olibugs' were born, later joined in *ZZAP!64* by game characters Rockford and Thing On A Spring. The text for the catalogue was typed on a small Smith Corona electric typewriter in a narrow column. The paper was then cut up and the strips stuck down with Cow Gum onto larger layout sheets. Oliver inked his illustrations straight onto the layouts, and in some examples it is possible to see the 'jump' where his pen nib bumped over the cut edge of a text column. The resulting four to eight pages then went down the road to a local Ludlow instant printer to run off several hundred copies for mailing.

Crash Micro Games Action was successful, and sales expanded. As a result of a PR campaign run in the local newspaper, Ludlow schoolboys began knocking at the front door after four o'clock, clutching fivers in their hands to purchase the latest releases. They became the nucleus of a reviewing pool, and subsequent issues of the catalogue carried more pertinent criticism written by the games' target audience. It was one of these copies that fell into the hands of a magazine distributor, who showed it to a buyer at W.H. Smith. The buyer was impressed, so the distributor rang Ludlow and said 'You can make this into a real magazine.'

The launch of Newsfield

It was September 1983. The partnership had just about enough money to get a first issue to press, but it would have to be in black and white, printed on newsprint paper, with a heavier weight colour cover. Would advertisers go for black and white? Most didn't mind too much, but W.H. Smith insisted that there should be at least 16 pages of colour inside and the projected 49p retail price was raised to 70p to cover the additional cost. (The first issue actually cost 75p, thanks to a last-minute increase in the cost of paper). At the same time, Frey, Frey and Kean dissolved the partnership in favour of a new limited liability company. Its 'off-the-shelf' name, Newsfield Limited, seemed appropriate, so it was never changed.

Kean spent most of October and November planning and writing articles for the first issue and organising reviews with the pool of eager

schoolboy reviewers, who earned modest fees for their services. Meanwhile, Franco Frey kept the mail order division going and Oliver set about creating the interior art and – most importantly – the cover. He had already adopted the Crash Micro Games Action logo with its squat, uncompromising, tank-like and completely unforgettable *CRASH* logo (keeping the 'Micro Games Action' as a sub-heading), but the image to go below it had to be outstanding.

At that moment no game suggested itself as something to illustrate, and besides, Oliver wanted an image that leaped out at the viewer and spoke volumes about the gaming experience without tying it to any particular game. Kean suggested a 'face' staring out at the potential reader with something like Space Invaders reflected in his eyes. Oliver sat down, sketched out a few ideas and then began air brushing and painting. The result is probably one of the most distinctive, certainly most famous, images ever created for a games magazine cover (*see page 39*). Since those days there have been many clever and more polished cover designs than that first *CRASH*, but none with the sheer brutal impact of the alien they came to call 'The Chairman of the Board'. Even today, its simple directness is overwhelming.

The first *CRASH* – the February issue – went on sale on Wednesday, 13 January 1984. It was more than moderately successful in sales, but hardly earth shattering. Issue 2, with another unforgettable cover – King Kong clutching a screaming girl, tearing into a Spectrum with his fangs (*see page 42*) – did better. Unfortunately, the nice distribution company went bankrupt, taking all the receipts from the first two issues with it. There was no money to pay the printer. Two things saved *CRASH*: in turn the printer went belly up (not because of *CRASH*), which bought breathing space, and Britain's biggest magazine distributor Comag, liking what they saw, picked up the distribution and managed to collect some of the owed money from the newstrade.

Thanks to Comag, Newsfield survived, and Oliver Frey continued to pour out an astonishing stream of cover and interior art for *CRASH*, then in 1985 for *ZZAP!64*, and on for some further ten magazines, as well as numerous game inlays for various software publishers. Oliver's involvement with the Newsfield story is legend to the publishing company's readership; less well known are the years of hard work that went into making him such a prolific and versatile illustrator.

Final pencil sketch for the *CRASH* logo and rough for the first mail order catalogue cover, dated June '83.

Portrait of Roger
Frey's painting of the author working on an oil painting with the London Film School as his subject.
Acrylics on canvas, signed *Oliver Frey '72*

The 'Chairman'
Frey's cover for the first issue of *CRASH* announced to the British gaming world that something new had arrived.

Family Frey
Oliver, Giulietta, Lauretta, Ugo and Franco (l-r).
Oil on hardboard
Roger Kean, 1972.

THE EARLY YEARS

A very accomplished watercolour from the 14-year-old Frey, signed 'Oli' and dated '62.

Eagle and Dan Dare – formative influences on many youngsters growing up in the late 1950s and early 60s.

Oliver Frey was born on 30 June 1948 in Zurich, Switzerland. He is the eldest of three children (two boys and a girl) born to Ugo and and Giulietta Frey. He grew up a fluent Italian speaker, since his parents hailed from the southernmost canton of Switzerland, Ticino, where Swiss-Italian is spoken. However, because the family lived near Zurich in the north, he also learned German and French at school. His artistic career really started in 1956, when he was almost eight, and the Frey family came to Britain from Switzerland, bringing their car with them on a Silver City air ferry. During the short flight from France a steward handed the puzzled boy a Dan Dare badge. It looked exciting, but who was Dan Dare, Pilot of the Future, and what did he do?

The answer was supplied almost immediately in the hotel they were lodged in while Ugo Frey's English employers found suitable housing for the family. Hidden under the cushions of a sofa in the residents' lounge, Oliver discovered copies of *Eagle* comic, and the badge and the *Dan Dare* strip matched up.

When he started school in Wembley, young Oliver discovered that most of his classmates were comic-mad, especially for *Eagle*. There had been no such comics in Switzerland, and he was taken by the quality of artwork, immersing himself in the deeds of Dan Dare and his battles with the Mekon. He started copying the drawings of *Eagle*'s artists and their styles became seminal influences. The feeling of bodies in movement, often in violent action, captured his imagination and is a quality that has never left his work.

11

Did he inherit his artistic abilities? 'I wouldn't say my family was particularly artistic, although my great-grandfather had been a painter of landscapes and portraits who'd made his way in the USA before retiring to a Swiss mountain valley. This had been well before my time, and only a couple of pieces of his work were extant. My family encouraged me to keep drawing, though.'

After a few years, the Frey family returned to Switzerland and in school Oliver had to relearn the German he had almost forgotten, having easily picked up English. An English friend of his parents continued to send him copies of *Eagle*, however, and a weekly dose of comic fun arrived in the post. On the due day of the week, Oliver – quite unable to wait for the postman to ring the bell and hand over the tightly rolled mailer – hovered outside the front door. He has ever been addicted to the post's arrival – a sense of fearing to miss out on anything, even today when most of it is junk mail. That feeling of eternal anticipation is also reflected in many of his best paintings, when the viewer senses that the artist has deliberately captured a moment just a split-second before something else interesting might happen.

Oliver admired the work of *Eagle* artists Frank Hampson (Dan Dare's creator), Frank Humphries and most particularly Frank Bellamy 'Frank Bellamy's line and colour work was so dramatic and action-packed. He was one of Britain's best comic strip artists. I also loved Eugene Delacroix, again for the drama!'

American comics played little part in his development as an illustrator. 'It was the British comics that were the mainstay, followed by French comic albums. American comics that spring to mind are old *Prince Valiants* (reprinted in Swiss magazines). The superhero comics were too over the top for my liking.'

The home-made comic album
On his return to school in Switzerland in the early 1960s, Frey continued to draw comic strips and began compiling entire hand-bound albums in the style of *Eagle*. This spread from the February–May 1965 album shows the conclusion of an episode of *Der Schwarze Dan* (Black Dan), a Wild West story, and the start of *Henry of the Skies* – which speaks for itself.
The albums switched freely between German and English, and as well as action-adventures included all the more serious articles and illustrated 'great lives' that had made *Eagle* such a worthy success.
The medium is ink and crayon.

A Vietnam experience
Undated, but probably executed in 1967, this ink and acrylic montage of Vietnam War images verges on the 'arty', but displays all the drama and strong composition of Frey's later work.

Influences, practice and a struggle for recognition

In 1966, Frey sent samples of artwork to his favourite comics in an attempt to be taken on as an illustrator. The example **above right** is a reworking of a page of *Dan Dare in the Menace From Jupiter*, which clearly shows his imitation of the dot-shading technique of Frank Bellamy (**far right**) combined with the fluid line of Frank Hampson (**right**), which he always preferred to the painterly style of Don Lawrence (**left**).

Oliver sent several of his own best drawings to his favourite comics, especially *Eagle*, then owned by Odhams Press Limited, but while encouraging (*see the side panel*), the responses were all in the negative. He was, however, once rewarded with a reply from *Look & Learn*'s Don Lawrence, the man from whom he would one day take over the *Trigan Empire* strip.

The lure of the movies

While drawing action figures was a vital part of his artistic development, the cinema was another formative influence. Typically, given his preference for drama and adventure, it was the James Bond movies that attracted Oliver the most. Using an 8mm camera, he directed his younger sister Lauretta and brother Franco in two lengthy films he scripted in English; the sound was dubbed on after editing. Playing both the parts of villain and hero 'Apple Apple Seven, James Tell', Oliver showed a natural flair for film-making. During the editing process, still frames exposed in the small edit-viewer also gave him a new perspective on figures in action. Gradually, Oliver began to move away from copying his comic artist heroes' pictures. The development of his own distinct style owes much to those editing stints, as he observed how arms, legs, hands and torsos flowed and moved when captured in 8mm still-motion.

While he was still at school, Oliver's attention was drawn to an advert for an American correspondence course in illustration called The Famous Artists. It was expensive, but he persuaded his parents to pay for it. The course comprised 36 lessons, written by a team of a dozen professional illustrators and contained in three huge volumes. Each lesson ended with an assignment, which had to be completed and sent off. Fortunately the cost of posting was reduced because the European edition of the course was run from Holland. Oliver has praised the quality of The Famous Artists ever since. Sadly, for today's aspiring illustrator, it has been long since defunct. From its invaluable lessons, the young illustrator learned about composition, use of materials, drawing, shading, colouring and most importantly the physical structure and articulation of the human body.

Failed film student, good corporal

Approaching the age of 18, a career in film making engaged Oliver's interest – realistically, he had little thought of earning a living from comic illustration, especially in Switzerland. After rejecting the respected film school in Munich ('all too serious and New Wave…') he flew to England and applied to the London Film School (then called the London School of Film Technique). The principal, Robert Dunbar, was interested but wondered whether Oliver's preference for action movies was quite what was needed, and advised that he was a little too young to start a course.

Disappointed, Oliver returned to Switzerland and began his compulsory army service, which lasted for three months of basic training

If at first you don't succeed…

In mid-1964, the art editor of Odhams Juvenile Publications (*Eagle*), John Jackson, wrote to Oliver: *'Thank you for your letter and your [Great War] sketch. I think your picture interpretations of the script is* [sic] *quite good, but the actual layout of the frames is a muddle. Finally, if you make your drawings half as big again on reduction you will find the result is much crisper.'*

Oliver tried again, and in September received a second letter: *'This strip is a great improvement on your previous work, but it is not yet good enough for use in our magazines. If it is possible for you to go to art classes for anatomy and perpecive, I think in a few years time you could start drawing professionally and eventually develop into a first class continuity artist.'*

The posters Oliver Frey created for his two 'Apple Apple Seven – James Tell' spy movies, filmed in glorious '8mm Kodachrome Colour', show an admiration for the art of James Bond. The second movie, *Operation Bloodsucker*, started before he left for the London Film School in January 1969, was only finished in January 1972, a year after completing the course – but in true Hollywood style, he did the poster before filming started.

In contrast to the film posters, two illustrated school Latin lessons (**above right and right**) experiment with classical children's illustration; a poster for a school production of Bach's *St. John's Passion* (**below**) plays with 'modernist' style; and a water colour (**bottom right**) shows that Frey's sense of the romantic was never far away.

Left: Proud in epaulets – Frey took his military national service in the Communications Corps seriously and became a corporal.

and three months work towards becoming a corporal. (At that time all Swiss men between the ages of 18 and the late forties were expected to report to barracks for a three-week period in the army every year after their basic training period). With his first military spell complete, Oliver began studying at Bern University, reading History, German Literature and English Literature with a vague view of entering the diplomatic service. Several of his older acquaintances felt he would be well suited to diplomacy, but obviously they had never encountered his flashes of intemperance when matters failed to go his way.

'Unfortunately, my university career wasn't a roaring success,' he recalls. 'I started going to the cinema seriously while I was at university, instead of going to lectures, and it wasn't long before I realised that I was much more interested in making films.'

After a term he left university and approached the London Film School again. 'This time I was accepted, and started a two-year course in 1969, which covered all aspects of film making.'

Right: A wraparound jacket for the 50th anniversary celebration magazine of SAIA, the Swiss company his father managed in the early 1970s, gave Frey an opportunity to try out cover illustration – the artform that would occupy most of his future output.

Above: This rare example of oil painting from Frey celebrates the Battle of Murten, which took place in 1476. The army of the Swiss Confederation defeated the forces of Charles the Bold of Burgundy on the edges of Lake Murten in Canton Fribourg. Switzerland was freed from Burgundian tyranny and the Duchy's power soon faded.
1968, oil on board; 147 x 77 cm, 58 x 30 in

'I did the most painting for its own sake when I lived with my parents in the town of Murten. The Battle of Murten *was my first attempt at a large-scale battle scene… and it shows.*

Christ on the Cross
1970, acrylics on shaped board and framed;
77 x 107 cm, 42 x 30 in

'I was brought up a Catholic, but lost any conviction in my early teens, so this was more an exercise in Gothic style, and the fun of the medieval shape.'

TURNING PROFESSIONAL

Unsupported by a British educational grant, for which he was deemed an ineligible 'alien', Oliver had to support himself. Illustration seemed to be the logical choice, so he looked for freelance comic work. He approached Fleetway (then independent of IPC) and was fortunate in meeting the editor of the War Picture Library series, E.J. Bensberg. 'A true hero of the back room,' Oliver later recalled of the man who, more than anyone, put him on the path to his future career. 'I persuaded Bensberg to let me illustrate a story so I could show him what I could do. I was given a script and told to go away and draw a five-page strip. He liked the result and I was commissioned to do a whole book.

'The books were small-format, 64-page, 150-frame, black and white picture-strip tales of World War Two. For two months, working in my Battersea bedsit during the evenings between mouthfuls of Heinz West End Grill heated on the single gas-ring, I pencilled and inked, and my first full story was accepted.' So began an association with the War Picture Library, which resulted in dozens of covers and illustrated stories before he stopped doing them in the mid-1970s.

Thanks to Bensberg keeping him busy, Oliver could potentially earn the then astronomical sum of £4,000 a year. At a time when an experienced school teacher could expect to earn not more than £1,700 per annum, this was astonishing – especially for a student. It was good fortune for Roger Kean, too. He had switched from studying fine art (painting) at Hornsey College of Art to the film school and joined the same course as Oliver. Kean was a more typical student – poor, by comparison to Oliver. The two got on well, agreed with many things, and agreed to disagree over Kean's 'arty' penchant for the films of Truffaut, Godard, Fellini and Pasolini. On his wealth, Oliver dined Kean well, and their film making at the school was the beginning of a working partnership that has survived the years.

Breaking the rules of war

'Once I started drawing War Picture Library stories, the thrill of finally being a published comic strip artist led to wanting to excel at the craft. Given the restricted size of the booklets, artists stuck rigidly to the 2-3-4 frames per page, all squared up; I wanted to add the excitement achieved in *Eagle* by my 'hero' Frank Bellamy with his dynamic picture frames and began breaking up my squared ones with the dramatic zig-zags he'd pioneered. I could, however, not apply the design features he created with his speech balloons as part of the whole composition: while he did his own lettering, text for my stories was added by a separate lettering artist and out of my control – all I could do was to leave suggestive spaces for balloons. Shame.'

The first two covers from Fleetways' War Picture Library series that Frey painted in early 1970. The war genre gave him a free rein on his love of figures in violent motion and vibrantly juxtaposed colours. *'I look at them today and shudder at how crude they appear, but the sheer number I churned out gave me the opportunity to experiment – as long as I remained within the editorial guidelines.'*

The apprentice

'Turning out more than 680 pages of War Picture Library in a space of eight years proved to be an invaluable foundation for later work.'

Detail from the front cover of a War Picture Library 'Holiday Special'.

The making of a British resident

Having completed the two-year film course by December 1970, Frey and Kean had to look to the future. The British film industry was going through one of its regular periods of decline – in fact it was in a dismal state – and the restrictive practices of the British film workers' union made it all but impossible for a foreign resident to break in anywhere. Oliver reluctantly returned to Switzerland, while Kean was offered an assistant film editor's job on a BBC Television golf series. Since the BBC did not recognise the film union, not having a 'union ticket' did not present him a problem. However, the plan was that Kean should move to Switzerland as soon as the editing job finished and form a documentary film company with Oliver, which he did a few months later.

The experiment was a failure. Oliver continued to support himself from his parents' home with comic strips for the War Picture Library, and by the beginning of 1972 Kean was back in England and editing films for the BBC and – finally as a union member – for independent commercial television companies.

In 1973, Oliver gained permission for a UK residency, so long as he would not be a drain on the welfare state, and he left Switzerland for good, settling in Highgate, North London. Throughout the 1970s Oliver established himself as a freelance comic artist, working on strips in IPC Comics' *Look & Learn* and its spin-off *Speed & Power*. Through the good offices of his agent, Temple Art's Pat Kelleher, other fields also opened up: somewhat lurid novel book covers for Souvenir Press, video inlay covers, lollypop wrapper designs for Walls and illustrations for children's book publishers, including Hamlyn, Usborne and Oxford University Press.

The yearning to direct films never went away. Early in 1975, Oliver spent a small fortune financing a ten-minute segment of a proposed feature film he had written with Kean. The film – *Blood of Satan* – was a *grand guignol* horror. They hired a small studio at Bushey and roped in Oliver's brother Franco to assist, with Denis Borrow, a friend from the London Film School, as cameraman. Three actors from the Central School of Drama who had helped out on film school exercises were paid a small fee to take part. Scenery was constructed from vast amounts of polystyrene, a large camera and lights hired, and shooting commenced, with Oliver directing.

The end result was a pretty polished movie, complete with specially commissioned music composed by an ex-schoolfriend of Kean's. Alas, *Blood of Satan* was to remain an interesting experiment. There was interest, despite its obvious flaws, but recent Hammer Horror movies had bombed at the box office and the old-fashioned genre was all but dead on its feet, overturned by the 1974 release of Tobe Hooper's grittily realistic and horrific *Texas Chainsaw Massacre*. Oliver returned to illustrating, Kean to editing films of the British Open and Wimbledon.

Thoughts in a Guinness
Oliver Frey in pensive mood, taking a crew break on 6 June 1969 while filming *Charlie Chaplin's London*, a student documentary exercise directed by Bill Douglas, who went on to direct *My Ain Folk*.

Left: *Blood of Satan*'s novelisation appeared in 1991, serialised in *Frighteners* magazine.

'Recce' at Doune
Roger Kean and Oliver Frey ponder some Polaroid stills during a reconnaisance at Doune Castle, Scotland, which had been used for the film *Monty Python and the Holy Grail*. They hoped to shoot *Blood of Satan* there, hence the trip north in the spring of 1974.

Right: Some stills from the 16mm filmstrip of *Blood of Satan*, directed by Frey, featuring actors Ian White, Ralph Lawton and Nigel Peagram.

Oil on board, Roger Kean, 1975

BARBARA MICHAELS
Black Rainbow

Various publishers kept Frey busy in the 1970s via the Temple Art Agency.
Left: Jacket design for *Black Rainbow*, a Souvenir Press novel. **Above:** 'The Tale of Sawney Bean' from the *Hamlyn Book of Horror*. **Right:** Interior page on the history of New Zealand in *Look and Learn*.
Below: A Scots-English battle in the Oxford University Press *Junior History*.

**'Vasco da Gama finds
the way around the
Horn'**
A fine example of Frey's
work for *Look & Learn*,
1977. Flipped
horizontally to suit the
text position, the
illustration was reused
for the title spread of
the book *Historical Atlas
of Exploration*,
published in 2000.

Three scenes from the *Hamlyn Book of Horror*, 1979.

Left: A drunken voodoo orgy.

Below: The story of two wolf children.

Facing: Poor Transylvanian peasants locked in and burned to death by Vlad the Impaler.

Below right: *The Soul Eater*'s jacket for Souvenir Press is an early example of Frey's use of the professional airbrush – that is one powered by a compressor rather than blowing the medium through a tube. It also presages the horror-romantic imagery that would later make *Fear* magazine covers so potent.

THE SOUL EATER
Robert Alexander

On the silver screen in 'letterbox'

In addition to regular work for the War Picture Library, a weekly strip came Oliver's way that he could hardly refuse. Some 17 years after receiving a letter of encouragement from Don Lawrence, the great man abandoned IPC Comics for more lucrative European pastures, and the art editor of *Look & Learn* asked Oliver to step into his shoes and paint *Trigan Empire*. It was, of course, flattering, but the chalice was tinged with poison. The brief was to slavishly reproduce Lawrence's famously painterly style. Oliver was more of a line-and-wash draughtsman.

'I do have admiration for Don's work, but I'm not really happy with the full-blown painting notion; it doesn't suit the gutsy verve of comics,' he complained. In fact, during this stint on *Trigan Empire*, having to paint the detail proved to be a useful discipline for Oliver. Some of this style can be seen in *The Terminal Man*, the comic strip he produced monthly for a year in first *CRASH* magazine and then *ZZAP!64*, albeit Oliver could not bring himself to abandon his beloved line undertones that give so much surface life to the artwork.

By the second half of the 1970s, Oliver's work was reaching a

Two of the two-page episodes of *Trigan Empire* drawn by Frey after he took over the prestigious comic strip from Don Lawrence; **below** from 1976, on the **right** from 1977. Frey used many acquaintances, as well as himself, as face models. The character appearing in the second-left frame on the bottom row in the 1977 strip bears a strong resemblance to the artist.

Right: An opening page of the weekly two-page black & white picture-strip adventures of *SOS International* which appeared in IPC Magazines' *Speed & Power* in 1975. *'This was my first "up-market" comics job, and while not in colour, the half-tone expanded my scope.'*

large audience – but one piece in particular reached a massive circulation. For *Superman, The Movie*, shooting at Pinewood Studios during late 1977, Oliver was brought in to design the film's opening sequence. While still prevented by union regulations from working in the British film industry, for his specialist skills an exception was made in this case. 'It was really a matter of luck. It turned out that the union's secretary – the real power – was a fan of my illustrations, and had mentioned my name to the film's art director. At first, they wanted me to work with the director of the film unit shooting Christopher Reeve's flying sequences, sketching out scenes derived from the bare shooting script.'

However, the very dynamic quality of Oliver's published illustrations condemned him to a lesser role. 'They were worried that the "flight" director was already going over budget, and exposing him to my imagination might prove ruinous. And that seemed to be that. But I got a call a few days later. It turned out that the film's director, Richard Donner, had decided to open the movie using an original comic strip, but none really suited his requirements. They needed someone to re-create the original style, but with frames that fitted what he wanted.'

Getting a title

These are photocopies of the comic strip Frey produced for *Superman the Movie* (the fate of the originals is unknown). The last two frames on the third page were left blank until after the model shot of the Daily Planet building had been filmed. The start frame of the zoom away from the building was sent to Frey so that he could match the last comic panel exactly for the dissolve from drawing to live-action film (the result seen **below**).

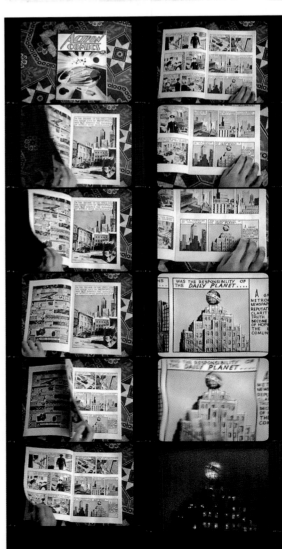

So, one afternoon a few days later Oliver found himself at Pinewood Studios, sitting outside Donner's office. His interview was somewhat delayed by the arrival of a gigantic cake – it was Donner's birthday. Then in a whirlwind brief, Donner sketched out his vision for the beginning. 'The idea was that you would be in a 1930s cinema, the curtains just opening to reveal a kid reading a Superman comic. The camera would zoom in on the pages, ending up on the Daily Planet building, at which point they would dissolve to the model shot of the "real" Daily Planet building. Dick [Donner] wanted me to produce some pencil roughs of a 1930s street scene "perhaps with a policeman swinging his nightstick…."'

Oliver returned two days later, with a pencil rough of the three-page strip and a comic cover inked in. 'In the Thirties, Superman was drawn in a very rough style, and I was worried that I might let myself down by copying the rough appearance of the originals. So I inked in the cover and held my breath while I handed over the work.'

He needn't have worried. Donner and his art director were impressed and the rough of the cover was accepted on the spot and used as it was in the title sequence, along with the finished version of the strip. 'It was a thrilling feeling to go to the Empire [in Leicester Square] the day after the premiere in 1978, together with Roger and Denis [Borrow, who had worked in Superman's camera department] and see my work flash up on that vast, luminous screen. Just a few short seconds – and that was that.'

Given his background in comic strips in combination with his interest in films, it would seem logical for Oliver to have become involved

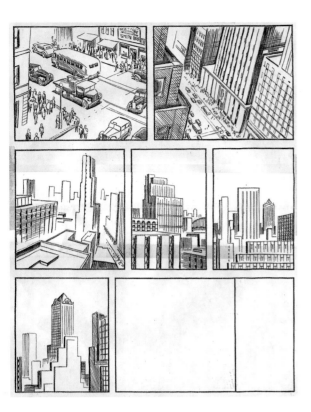

with animated movies. However, in an interview given in 1985, he refuted this notion. 'I do like animated films, but I've never been tempted to get involved with them. I'm not really very patient. When it comes to animation, there's so much work involved that I'm sure I couldn't put up with it. I've looked at the "old" process, and gave up the idea of making cartoon films before stalling. So much of the work is mechanical, tracing hundreds and hundreds of cells and inking them all in – I simply wouldn't be able to apply myself to such a task. And I couldn't sit down in front of a computer and fiddle endlessly with the keyboard to produce the result I wanted. Though if I had a team of animators at my disposal, to do all the finicky work....'

A different calling

While it is not in the scope of this book, the description of Oliver's early years as an illustrator would not be complete without at least mentioning his work for gay magazines in the last half of the 1970s. It has a different fanbase to that for his comic and video games art – though not exclusively so – and one which is no less admiring of the witty and erotic comic strips he produced during the period. It would be normal for anyone working in such separate fields to create a pseudonym for one of them, but typically Oliver found the idea unacceptable and signed the gay art with his own name: 'It seemed necessary, to do my bit for the gay cause as it fought for recognition during the Seventies.'

Among his output were several huge event posters for the new club at Charing Cross called Heaven, all of which were avidly collected by David Hockney, among other notable fans. His enthusiasm for the dramatic also led to involvement in directing several huge events at Heaven. In the most spectacular – a 'Roman' night – those packing the dance floor gasped in amazed horror as a 20-foot high Roman temple constructed from large TV boxes and rolled corrugated paper as column drums was made to collapse onto them.

Left: One of the several posters Frey produced for Heaven in the late 1970s. This advertised The Cellar bar in Heaven's basement.

Right: The illustrator in contemplative mood; the lure of London's bright lights was waning and Frey was considering a move to the country.

Detail from an unfinished oil painting on hardboard, Roger Kean, 1979

MICRO GAMES ACTION

The original *CRASH* magazine masthead, complete with 'Olibugs'.

CRASHING INTO THE BIGTIME

The year before his brief work on *Superman*, Oliver had visited the small market town of Ludlow in Shropshire, together with Roger Kean. Ralph Lawton, a graduate of the Central School of Drama, who had acted in one of their film school exercises and then in *Blood of Satan*, was appearing in a production of *Hamlet* during Ludlow's renowned arts festival, with its centrepeice of a Shakespeare play performed in the castle. To see the play was a reasonable enough excuse for a trip out of London. The summer of 1976 was a memorable one – so hot that a Michael Winner film scheduled to be shot in Spain ended up being made in parched and sun-blasted England, since no one could tell the difference in the landscape. It was hard not to fall in love with the medieval town under such conditions.

After many more visits, Oliver moved to Ludlow in October 1982. It just so happened that his parents – who had returned to England in the mid-1970s – and brother Franco were looking to move from the Home Counties, and early in 1983 an exodus to Ludlow took place. Franco, who had gained a degree in Engineering since his days of acting in James Tell movies and had worked on a variety of high-tech engineering projects for his father's UK-based company, became involved with a German firm which wanted to import Spectrum software from England. Franco exchanged his ZX81 for a Spectrum and was busily playtesting games, researching the market for his German contact, when he came up with the idea of starting a magazine – or at the very least, a mail order service selling Spectrum Software – which is where we came in on page 8.

Between 1984–1991, Oliver worked non-stop for his own company on Newsfield's stable of magazine titles. They were *CRASH* (for the Spectrum), *ZZAP!64* (Commodore 64), *Amtix!* (Amstrad), *The Games Machine* (multi-format), *LM* (an innovative 'laddish' lifestyle monthly that proved too in advance of the times to succeed) and *Fear*. For this last, hugely influential periodical – but sadly short-lived due to the demise of Newfield – Oliver created some of his most extraordinary cover illustrations. *Fear* spawned a spin-off called *Frighteners*, a collection of short horror stories by new writers, several of whom went on to become noted novelists. The first issue's cover illustrated the lead story by Graham Masterton, titled *Eric the Pie*. It was typical 'in-your-face'

Editor
Roger Kean

Designer
Oliver Frey

Consultant editor
Franco Frey

Staff writers
Lloyd Mangram
Rod Bellamy

Advertisement manager
John Edwards

Production designer
Michael Arienti

© 1984 Newsfield Ltd.

Crash Micro is published monthly by *Newsfield Ltd.*
PO Box 10, Ludlow,
Shropshire SY8 1DB
Tel: 0584 5620

No material may be reproduced in whole or in part without written consent from the copyright holders.

Mono printing, typesetting & finishing by
Feb Edge Litho Ltd.
3-4 The Oval, London E2.
Colour printing by
Allan-Denver Web Offset Ltd.
Northfield, Milton Keynes.
Colour origination by
Scan Studios, 44 Wallace Rd.
London N1
Distributed by
Wells Gardner, Darton & Co.
Faygate, Horsham, W. Sussex
Tel: 029383 444

Subscriptions: 12 issues £9.00
UK Mainland (post included)
Europe: 12 issues £15 (post included).
Single copy: 75p

If you would like to contribute to CRASH please send articles or ideas for projects to the above address. Articles should be typed. We cannot undertake to return them unless accompanied by a stamped addressed envelope.

Cover illustration: Oliver Frey

Frey's first home in Ludlow, 85 Old Street, was the place where *CRASH* was born and the first three issues laid out. *'It cost £30,000 at a time when a similar house in London was going for over £80,000.'*

The imprint details from issue 1 of *CRASH*.

The Eagle has crashlanded…

'By the time I got to draw my favourite character, Dan Dare, in 1983, his facial features had been "modernised" out of all recognition. The weekly comic he appeared in was

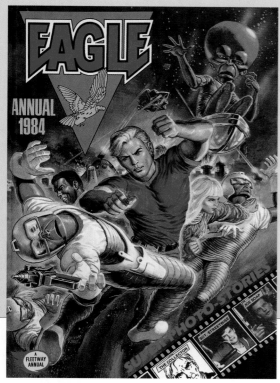

Below: The centrefold strip of Dan Dare in the 5 November 1983 issue of *Eagle*, typical of the poor reproduction. The *Eagle Annual* covers for 1984 and 1985 promised better fare.

printed on the cheapest of pulp paper, so true four-colour printing was impossible; I had to draw the story in black and white line, and someone at the printers added simple colour to it without any input from me. The result was pretty awful…

Relaunched in 1982 after its demise in 1969, once great *Eagle* was now a travesty.'

Frey, but so revolting to managers at W.H. Smith that the company had it removed from their store shelves. As a result, very few people ever got to see it, but it is reproduced in this book in all its gory glory (*see page 121*). The issue of *Frighteners* was re-published in the following month… with a suitably subdued cover illustration.

'I did 99 percent of the front covers and countless internal illustrations for all our games magazines,' Oliver recalls, 'literally hundreds of covers over the years.'

He did not work entirely exclusively for Newsfield. Twenty years after first sending samples of his youthful artwork to *Eagle*, Oliver was finally given the chance to work on the one comic strip above all others that had inspired him as a boy – Dan Dare. Sadly, the experience was less than wonderful (*see the panel above*), but it did drive him to greater efforts on Newfield's own comic, *The Terminal Man*:

'I had always planned a comic strip for *CRASH* [it reappeared in *ZZAP!64*]. It was written by *2000AD* author Kelvin Gosnell, illustrated by me, and it ran over four pages each month for 12 issues, detailing the adventures of Cross, the hero. When the first complete story concluded and issue 13 of *CRASH* appeared without *The The Terminal Man*, there was an outcry from hundreds and hundreds of readers. Kelvin was tied up on another commission so I started writing the second series myself. I even drew and inked in the first four pages, but it was obvious that the pressure of time on me once (continued on page 36)

THE LINER **ARCADIA** DID NOT EXPLODE IN AN EAR-SPLITTING **WHITE BANG** —

— THERE WAS NO AIR TO FUEL THE EXPLOSION OR CARRY THE SOUND‚‚‚

‚‚‚SHE BURNED WITH THE COLOUR OF **BLOOD** — FIERCELY AND SILENTLY CONSUMING HERSELF WITH HER OWN INTERNAL AIR‚‚‚

WHEN SHE HIT THE PLANET'S ATMOSPHERE SHE CARVED A PRETTY FIREWORK DISPLAY IN THE NIGHT SKY —

MINUTES LATER HER REMAINS TORE A GREAT SCARRED FURROW IN THE PLANET'S SURFACE‚‚‚

SHE HAD BEEN A BIG LINER, HER TAIL SECTION HIT AT A SHALLOW ANGLE —

The first episode of *The Terminal Man* is reproduced here, not as it first appeared in *CRASH*, but rescanned from the original boards and text overlays, lettered by Frey.

— MIRACULOUSLY **SOME** PASSENGERS SURVIVED‚‚‚

‚‚‚AND SET ABOUT TRYING TO **STAY** ALIVE —

ANYONE SEEN A MEDIKIT?

33

35

ZZAP!64 started would make it impossible to produce a monthly strip.'

However, it was not quite the end of the popular comic. Oliver kept trying to find the time, but it was not until 1987 that readers welcomed its return in issue 40 of *CRASH*. But by this time, Newsfield's titles had grown and the art demands on Oliver's time again proved too much. Skipping one month, *The Terminal Man* just stopped dead in its tracks in issue 44, with the words 'Next Month: Anchor in Space'. The second series of *The Terminal Man* has remained one of comics' great unfinished masterpieces.

In the later 1980s, Newsfield branched out into software publishing with its own games label, Thalamus. The company produced several high-quality games for the Commodore 64 computer, and Oliver created several of the cover inlay illustrations (David Rowe did the second Thalamus game, *Delta*). The first concern, however, was a logo. The thalamus is a gland set at the base of the brain and top of the spine, resonsible for sensation and feelings, a suitable name for a games publisher, but how to present it visually? The result was a striking abstraction of a face, retaining the shape of the letter T. 'I wanted something that indicated sensitivity with a determination to win, and an eye gazing into a distant, imagined future, or past.'

Thalamus Games was later sold, and at some point afterwards ceased to operate. Years later, Oliver revived his logo artwork for his own book publishing company.

End of one era, start of another

At the height of Newsfield's success, Oliver was jointly responsible for directing the operations of some 60-plus staff working the three separate buildings around Ludlow. In 1989 the whole firm was brought together in new offices sited in a renovated water mill on the banks of the River Teme. Unfortunately, the move proved to be a poor omen. Newsfield went into liquidation in September 1991, the result of the downturn in the first generation computer games boom and a failure to turn the publishing company into something bigger. But it was far from the end of Oliver's magazine illustration career. Within five weeks, he was back at work for a new organisation. The Macclesfield-based publisher Europress bought Newsfield's assets, rehired many of the staff and launched Impact Magazines Limited in Newfield's former premises. *CRASH* and *ZZAP!64* returned, the former soon sold to publishing giant EMAP, the latter converted to a new, more compact magazine named *Commodore Force*.

Two new titles were launched, *Sega Force* for the Mega Drive games console (Genesis in the USA) and *SNES Force* for the Super Nintendo. For *Sega Force*, Oliver produced a series of stunning posters. The interior art (the covers mostly went to pre-made art from the software publishers of games) was strongly influenced by Japanese manga-animé; the magazine's style was set in 'Neo-Tokyo'. The posters were published

Right: For teenaged boys all over Britain, 2 King Street, Ludlow became a place of pilgrimage. The three floors above Victoria Wine – today taken by Barclays Bank – were a sweatshop of innovative magazine publishing.

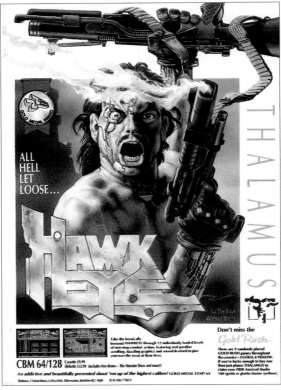

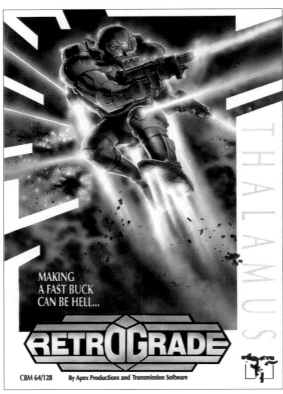

in two or three parts over several months and designed to stick together. They were a great success, and appear in this book joined together.

In March 1994, Oliver, together with Roger Kean and Franco Frey, left Impact to again form their own company. 'We slowly moved away from magazines and began producing books for publishers like Virgin and Carlton Books; initially games guides, but then on into music and sports. A year later, we were acquired by Prima, an American publisher, and that enabled us to expand. In 1997 we started what is called co-edition publishing, where we create a book for international publishers – mainly historical reference for the family market. I do all the illustration work that is not photographic.'

California-based Prima suffered badly when the 'dotcom' bubble burst in the late 1990s and cut back on its European arms. Oliver, Franco Frey and Roger Kean engineered a management buy out of the books division, and again set up on their own, 'We were thinking of names for the new company, and remembered Thalamus Games, long defunct. I had always liked my logo, so we used it, and Thalamus Publishing [the publisher of this book] came into being.'

In 2004, Oliver commenced work on a massive undertaking for Thalamus. 'I persuaded Roger to write a complete history of all the Roman emperors, and claimed I could find a portrait of every one to illustrate it.' And he did.

The result is *The Complete Chronicle of the Emperors of Rome*, for which Oliver illustrated 380 men, women and children, all drawn from portraits taken from coins or busts of the people featured.

The way that Oliver produces his artwork has changed over the years. There was a time when he asserted that he would never abandon traditional methods in favour of computer-generated art, but the illustrations for the *Emperors of Rome* were all produced on an Apple Macintosh. At the end of this book there is a section on his art techniques, which covers everything from pen and brush to Photoshop airbrush. In between, the pages are devoted to a gallery of Oliver Frey's fantasy art – some never before seen in print – free of the cover lines, logos and free gifts of the magazine days. It is an opportunity to look again at some of the finest action images from this unique, talented illustrator who claims to be no artist.

Thalamus success
Newsfield games software enjoyed great popularity with reviewers and players, and Frey wanted to help boost them with a series of fresh-looking inlay designs.

1 | MONSTERS AND ALIENS

'If we ever doubted what we were talking about, Oliver Frey's magnificent covers painted the reality for us – one day, we knew, the [game] graphics would really look like this.'

Roger Kean in The DEF Tribute to ZZAP!64

'Oliver Frey was invaluable, incredible. Most of his illustration work was off the cuff. He'd just do it. There were always awkward spaces to fill and he'd knock up suitable imagery in minutes.'

Gary Penn in The DEF Tribute to ZZAP!64

Given the predominance of videogames which involve battling against aliens from space or monsters of the id, it comes as no surprise that a great deal of Oliver Frey's work for magazine covers, interior art and posters is populated by images of weird creatures.

CRASH #1 cover
November 1983

'What we wanted for cover one was a slick but iconic look. This mix of Alien and Darth Vader was given relevance by having the creature enjoying a shoot-'em-up – a Roger Kean idea (like so many), if I recall… It took me a whole week to airbrush and paint – well worth it, as it turned out. We later nicknamed him "The Chairman of the Board", because it seemed as though he had brought us great luck and led on to the success of Newsfield. I remember having to travel down to London with the finished board to have it photographed (no one in Ludlow could produce A4-sized transparencies for reproduction) and then take the tranny to our London-based scanning house to go under the repro camera. This was long before the days of electronic scanning!'

A new era of videogame entertainment began on Wednesday, 13 February 1984, when CRASH issue 1 went on sale. Frey's artwork of an alien playing *Space Invaders* was a sensation with a growing fan base crying out for a serious games magazine.

SEGA FORCE #4
Contents page illustration
February 1992

'The magazine's art style was influenced by cult anime Akira and set in anarchic Neo-Tokyo: we wanted to shock.'

CRASH #15
'Get a Bite of Britain's Brightest Spectrum Games Mag!'
February 1985

'After a few covers tied to particular games, I had the freedom again to interpret a sales slogan. The notion of having an alien monster wearing complex head gear with two Spectrum keyboards as headlights came from seeing the matrix of semi-transparent keys glow when my brother had taken one apart to clean the computer and they were caught in the glare of a lamp. The main difficulty was to get the area around the alien's head really dark so the lights would glow brightly, and yet keep sufficient detail in the shadow behind to make out the structure of the equipment.'

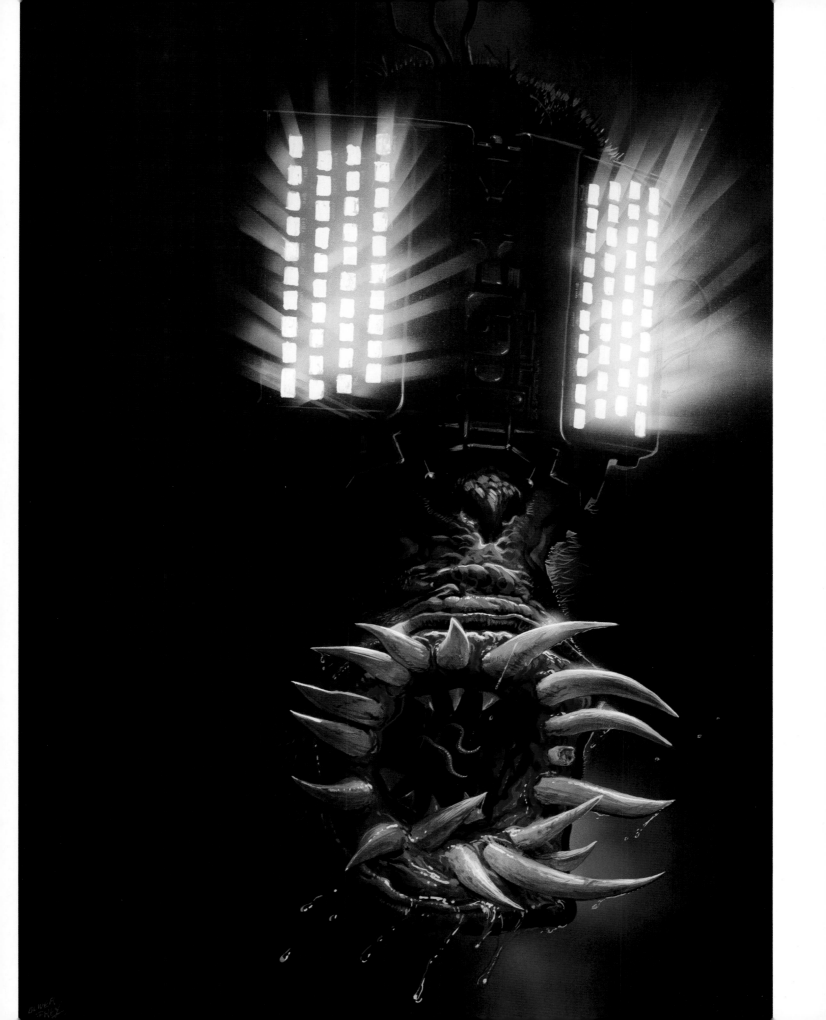

Previous pages:
CRASH #2 cover 'Kong'
January 1984

ZZAP!64 #2 cover
'Wipe Out – Theatre Europe'
April 1985

'The follow-up cover to the "Chairman of the Board" was critical. It had to have an equal impact and yet the first issue of CRASH had not even hit the shops when I started painting this one, so we had no feedback to go on. Versions of "Kong" were popular on arcade machines, and the idea of the beast taking it out on a Spectrum seemed natural enough.'

CRASH #20 cover
'Red Moon'
July 1985

Opposite:
CRASH #24 poster
October 1985

'The use of orbs – sun, moon – as a major compositional feature: they help create an monumental, epic scale.'

© NEWSFIELD PUBLICATIONS 1985

ZZAP!64 #18 cover
'Beyond the Forbidden Forest'
August 1986

'While being a legitimate depiction of a moment in the game, ZZAP!64 reviewers Julian Rignall and Gary Penn egged me on to plumb the situation's all too obvious "depths".'

AMTIX! #9 cover
'The Fifth Axis'
May 1986

'An example of how lighting and composition can liven up a standard action scene.'

ZZAP!64 #10 cover
'The Eidolon'
December 1986

*'How gloom and an
eery glow can
transform "cutesy"
creatures into
something altogether
more menacing.'*

ZZAP!64 #77 cover
'Rubicon'
July 1991

**ZZAP!64 #100
(COMMODORE FORCE #10)
centrefold poster 'The
Monstrous Force of Games'**
August 1993

**ZZAP!64 #34 poster
'Predator'**
December 1987

*'Arnie
Schwarzenegger's film
was a big hit, and its
use of computer
graphics for the alien
predator's eye-vision
was nicely adapted in
the game.'*

*'Note the contrast
between full-on
dramatic light effects
(opposite) and the much
more mysterious
atmosphere (left), which
is quite traditionally
painterly – and took a
lot longer to complete.'*

CRASH #9 cover
**'Backpacker's Guide to the
Universe'**
August 1984

CRASH #24 Christmas Special cover
November 1985

'Christmas issues were usually an excuse for cuddly fun – not my favourite theme, but you have to try; humour always helps.'

CRASH #35 cover 'Cobra'
September 1986

'A typical example of my spittle-spraying fiends: for me, the illustrator's life was never the same again after Ridley Scott's Alien.'

2 | SPACE MANOEUVRES

From the very beginnings of the videogame boom, the most popular game type involved the player shooting at an adversary. From the simplicity of 'Space Invaders' and 'Asteroids' to the horizontally scrolling 'Defender' action in which the player's craft progressed over an increasingly hostile landscape, shoot-'em-ups, as they became known, represented the most addictive of games. In the early days, when the graphics were little more than primitive sprites suggesting the craft, aliens and laser-beam weapons, shoot-'em-ups set in space were the games that asked most of the player's imagination. Oliver Frey always thought it was his task in life to bring them to life, providing exciting visuals that the games so often lacked.

**CRASH #28 cover
'Samantha Fox and
Starstrike II'**
March 1986

'Phallic spacecraft, brilliant con-trails and bursting explosions combined with a dreamy girl make a rather obvious image, but it requires the right frame of mind…'

The editorial brief was simple enough: make something out of *Samantha Fox Strip Poker* and *Starstrike II*. It was an inhibiting notion, and one which Frey left till he could no longer avoid doing the illustration. With this cover, a very popular one, it is the strength and dynamism of the composition that makes it work at all. He was pleased with the effect, but in general he hated the illustration and felt it was rather like a poorly-licensed game – the subject was unsuitable for an exciting picture.

So said the editorial in January 1988's CRASH History feature, but the image is an enduring one.

Opposite:
CRASH #5 cover
'Into the Trench'
April 1984

'We were still trying to avoid the covers of CRASH becoming tied to a specific game, while putting the reader in the thick of the gaming experience. Someone suggested an image inspired by the "trench" sequence from Star Wars, *and it was Roger Kean who said "make the trench from stacks of Spectrum game cassette boxes".'*

CRASH #21 cover
'Astro Clone'
August 1985

**ZZAP!64 #30 cover
'The Shoot 'Em Up
Construction Kit'**
August 1987

*'I spent days on this,
wanting to produce my
best-ever hardware SF
image. The misty
atmospherics may not
conform to the airless
reality of space, but it
was the romance of
interstellar exploration I
aimed to conjure.'*

CRASH #98 cover
February 1992

*'The last ever CRASH
cover I painted. The
exploding world aptly
conveys the feelings of
everyone who worked
on the magazine at the
time.'*

**Following pages:
ZZAP!64 #87 centre-spread
poster 'Readers' Charts'**

*'A multi-purpose
background painting,
this is a generic
"apocalyptic" shoot-
'em-up scene.'*

AMTIX! '#0' cover
August 1985

'The editor wanted an image of an exploding computer. This was intended only for the launch publicity, but I reworked the idea for the first issue's front cover [see index, page 190]. *The launch cover art did find itself put to use again, however, as the cover of issue 18 (April 1987).'*

CRASH #16 cover
'Sportscene Roundup'
March 1985

'A sports-simulation feature in May's issue meant the cover's topic wasn't in question, but the problem was how to portray the subject without a trite sports montage. I turned the idea on its head, creating a footballer, his body made up of recognisable sporting equipment, booting a spaceship towards the onlooker.'

Remarkably, the picture was painted in only three to four hours while Frey fitted in his new commitment to ZZAP!64.

ZZAP!64 #31 cover
'Hunter's Moon'
September 1987

'I had to leave a lot of space for the cover feature advertising a 3D section, complete with representation of the the 3D glasses which were included.'

These two covers show how Frey frequently had to accommodate awkward editorial 'sell lines' in the composition. The example on the left has the larger area of 'dead' space, but Frey's vigorous airbrushing only emphasises the cinematic sense of the craft's speed.

ZZAP!64 #42 cover
'Katakis'
August 1988

ZZAP!64 #35 cover
'Apollo 18'
January 1988

'I remember having to finish the astronaut in a bit of a rush before going to the Philippines on the first holiday I'd taken since Newsfield started up. It was only while flying above Vietnam that I suddenly realised that the ZZAP!64 logo seen in the faceplate reflection should have been reversed – by which time it was too late to do anything about it, since no one had mobiles in those days. As it turned out, everyone thought it was deliberately intended, just another quirk of the magazine's humour.'

'Snare'
game box artwork for
Thalamus Games
1989

*See the printed version
with added gridlines on
page 37*

'Heatseeker'
game box artwork for
Thalamus Games
1990

'Imbuing a silly-looking character with intriguing quirkiness.'

3 | MECHANICAL MAYHEM

Oliver Frey's image of a recognisable but gigantic joystick rampaging through a *Terminator*-like gloom, looming above the ant-like humans attacking it, was iconic and set the stage for a series of images featuring mechanical destructiveness – robotic, humanoid or cyborg. No less impactive are the more 'normal' pictures of hurtling jets, helicopters and madly driven vehicles.

CRASH #3 interior art
'Sub Track'
March 1984

A typical example of 'space filling' from the Spectrum Games Guide. The shape Frey had to fill was determined by the layout of the text. Comic-style line art like this was inked directly onto the layout sheets, often minutes before the pages had to go to the printer.

CRASH #10 cover
'Battlefield Joystick'
September 1984
Collection of Mrs. S.M. Kean

'Joysticks for the ZX Spectrum were a relatively new phenomenon – mostly players manipulated the sprites onscreen by use of the Speccy's infamous rubber keys. But by the tenth issue, several manufacturers (including my father) had developed plug-in joysticks, enough for a roundup, which we called "Battlefield Joystick". The title seemed to immediately suggest the cover's subject matter.'

ZZAP!64 #7 cover
'Paradroid'
September 1985

'The editorial team was mad for this new game, "Paradroid", and its programmer – Andrew Braybrook – supplied detailed information as to how the final robot would look in time for me to knock up the cover picture.'

CRASH #87 cover 'Hydra'
February 1991

Following pages:
COMMODORE FORCE #9
poster 'Gunship'
July 1993

'I always loved the Apache gunship – at the same time brutally ugly and graceful. It resembles a maddened insect out for blood.'

SEGA FORCE MEGA #V2.3
cover 'Thunderhawk'
August 1993

'How to make the ubiquitous chopper, so favoured by games designers, look different and arresting.'

CRASH #80 cover
'RoboCop 2'
July 1990

'I did a lot of RoboCops for our magazines – this was a particularly action-packed one…'

ZZAP!64 #76 cover
'Turbocharge'
June 1991

'Creating action scenes with the cinematic feel of motion and speed is quite a challenge. If your painting is too polished the picture becomes static; plenty of smoke, dust and debris brings events to life.'

CRASH #51 cover
'Cybernoid'
January 1988

AMIGA FORCE #11 cover
'Combat Air Patrol'
September 1993

CRASH #49 cover
'Flying Shark'
December 1987

'I love aircraft, and it was a pleasure to be able to paint this vintage aerial combat scene – a rare subject for a videogame.'

ZZAP!64 #8 cover
'Redhorn the Terrible meets the Mighty Zoidzilla'
October 1985

ZZAP!64 #68 cover
'Chase HQ 2'
October 1990

CRASH #94 calendar
October 1991

(Also used in close up as the cover for ZZAP!64 #79, December 1991)

'Futuristic armour and weaponry gone mad!'

**'Retrograde'
game box artwork for
Thalamus Games**
1989

'Knowing that the final layout would probably obscure my signature if I placed it near to the bottom [see page 36], I decided to give the blaster he's firing my name.'

4 | THE GAMING EXPERIENCE

During the 1980s and early 1990s, Oliver Frey painted many magazine covers and posters that, in a variety of ways, portrayed the gaming experience. He was for ever trying to propel the viewer into an imaginative confrontation with the particular game's nature or into a state of gaming ecstasy.

COMMODORE FORCE #8 poster
June 1993

'The intent behind this poster was to make the experience of playing video games very visceral. I wanted it to be gritty and – within the bounds of fantasy – very realistic.'

Game poster 'Joystick Boy'
July 1993

'This is only part of the actual printed poster. I painted it so that it could be stitched into the cover image of an older ZZAP!64 magazine [see page 46], making it seem as though the blithely playing youngster is about to be swallowed by the space worm.'

AMIGA FORCE #2 posters
Both January 1993

'What is important in these two posters is that – unlike the one on the previous page – the game characters are helping the players to win and not attacking them. One commands a spaceship, the other has his bullets, and each boy is entranced by aliens or heroes – and in the process becoming a part of the games they are playing.'

CRASH #4 cover
'What Now?'
March 1984

This example of
including gaming
elements into the image
– in this case the feel of
playing an adventure
game – was another of
Frey's early *CRASH*
covers with a face
staring straight out at
the prospective reader.
The first Spectrum text
adventure games
generally led the player
into a typical quandary
and posed the question
'What Now?' The 'L'
was the Spectrum
cursor symbol that
prompted the
player to type in
a command.

CRASH #25 cover
'Mikie'
December 1985

*'I was not overly thrilled
with the concept for this
"Valentine" game cover
image but, oddly, it has
remained one of the
more popular images.'*

**ZZAP!64 #12 cover
'Wild Sounds'**
February 1986

*'The major feature in
this issue was titled
"Wild Sounds From the
C64" and the inspiration
for the picture came
from the amazing video
for Duran Duran's track
Wild Boys.'*

**Following pages:
ZZAP!64 #9 1985
and AMTIX! #15 1986
Christmas Specials**
November 1985 and
November 1986

In the Zzap edition, the
magazine's two game
mascots (Rockford and
Thing) watch a Pet
Person (another game
character, a portrait of
its creator David Crane
on the wall) playing,
while editorial writers
Gary Penn and Julian
Rignall look in through
the window. AMTIX!'s
cover features the
editorial team (Malcolm
Harding, Anthony
Clarke, Richard Eddy
and Massimo Valducci)
largely ignoring the
monster breaking in
behind.

CRASH #13 cover
December 1985

One of the most striking
images from early
CRASH resulted from
the use of a black-and-
white photograph of a
competition reader who
visited Newsfield and
posed specifically for a
cover. Frey retained the
monochrome to
heighten the Spectrum's
logo colours.

Opposite:
**ZZAP!64 #23 cover
'With Zzap!64 You're
Always Part of the Action!'**
January 1987

SEGA FORCE #4 cover
'Kid Chameleon'
February 1992

The Sega machines brought a new level of visual realism to game graphics. 'Chameleon' told the story of a young man who could change into several different heroic characters, each with their own unique strengths and weaknesses.

SEGA FORCE #13
calendar poster
November 1992

'When we first formulated Sega Force, *I wanted to give it a distinct visual feel in which the entire magazine became steeped in the Japanese gaming phenomenon – it was a new gaming experience. The model for this was the animé* Akira, *which was set in a future city called Neo Tokyo. In this world, everyone goes about armed to the teeth – or at least, they did in* Sega Force.'

Following pages:
Two Neo Tokyo 'Game Freak Alley' posters
left (rotated):
SEGA FORCE #s 3, 4, 5
March–May 1992;
right (rotated):
SEGA FORCE #s 7, 8
July–August 1992

'These posters were made up of several centrefolds, designed to be stuck together by the reader. In fact they gave me a technical problem because the originals were longer than a standard piece of artboard, so I had to do some sticking together as well…'

SEGA FORCE #s 10, 11 poster
'Neo Tokyo Battle'
August 1992

Right: SEGA FORCE #16 poster
'You're just a slimy scumbag alien to be stamped on! Get it?'
February 1993

COMMODORE FORCE #6
poster 'The Games Thinker'
April 1993

*'This argues that
joystick virtuosity has to
combine with brain
power to win in the
Commodore games
world.'*

5 | SPORTING TYPES

'Baseball Bud'
One of the reguar characters who appeared in *Nintendo Force* magazine, 1991–92.

'I posed the editorial team according to a rough pencil sketch I'd done previously. The photograph was scanned in, and after I'd painted the fictional characters – including Bud as seen here on his own – I stitched the elements together in Photoshop.'

CRASH #8 cover
'Spectrum Diver'
July 1984

'A Spectrum gamer's bliss – diving into a pool reflecting the computer keyboard.'

Sporting themes were – and still are – a popular basis for video games. Oliver Frey's contribution ranged from the (almost) literal depiction of a game's content to abstract ideas and good old-fashioned mayhem in extreme activities.

ZZAP!64 #15 cover
'Leader Board'
May 1986

'The theme for this cover was US Gold's golfing game "Leader Board". The obvious image would have been a golfer teeing off, but shortly before I had to commit to painting something, a rival C64 magazine's publisher – who considered his own title a serious gamer's periodical compared to ours – referred to ZZAP! as a "fluffy lollypop rag". This was our response. I liked its cheek so much that it still hangs on my wall.'

ZZAP!64 #29 cover
'California Games'
July 1987

ZZAP!64 #71 cover
'Super Monaco Grand Prix'
January 1991

'The cover-mounted cassette of four free games ate up so much space on this cover that I opted for having the "Grand Prix" girl offer it up as a sign board.'

CRASH #19 cover
June 1985

'This cover celebrated the all-singing, all-dancing 64K Spectrum, expanded thanks to a new peripheral, which surfed in with real, solid keys!'

THE FANTASY ART OF OLIVER FREY

ZZAP!64 #39 cover
'Skate Crazy'
May 1988

Opposite:
CRASH #61 poster
'Skateball'
December 1988

'The ice rink's eery glow highlights the game's violent nature.'

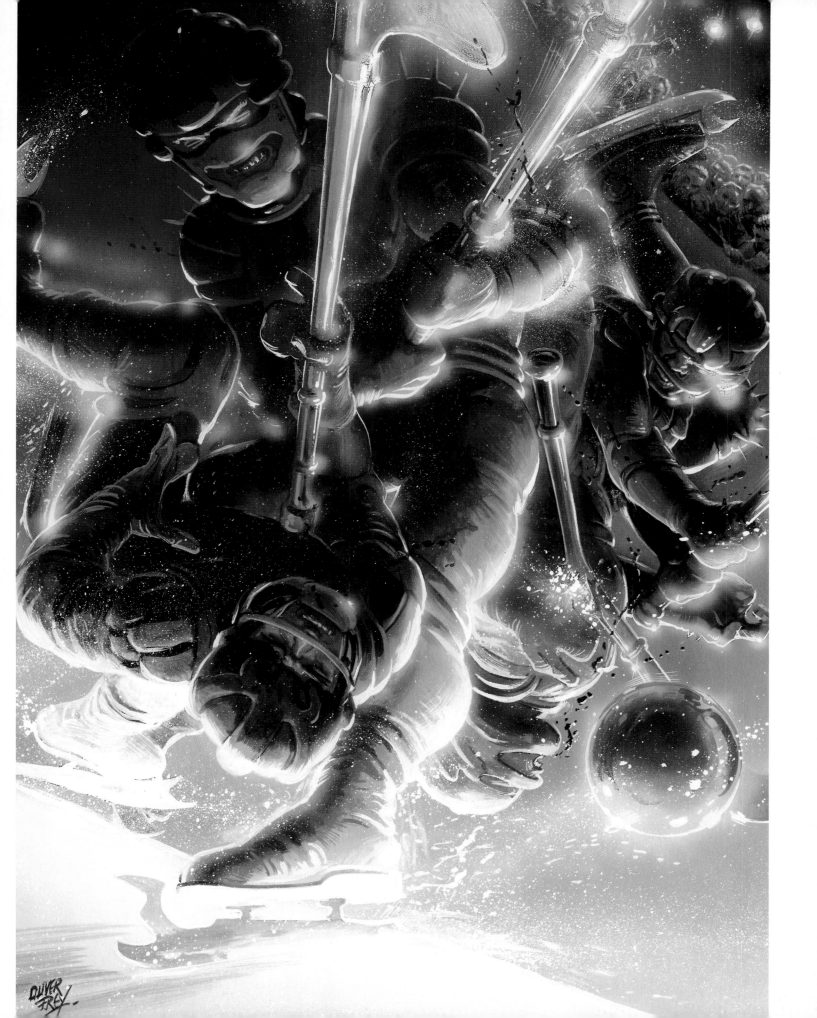

CRASH #79 cover
'Gladiator'
June 1990

'All the action of the arena a decade before Russell Crowe trod the sand…'

ZZAP!64 #87 cover
'American Sports'
June 1992

Street Fighter II
Two backgrounds for the Merlin-TOPPS sticker album of 1993.

'The trick with these was to compose scenes that would survive when the stickers were plastered all over them.'

ZZAP!64 #50 cover
'Speedball'
April 1989

6 | GRUE AND GORE

Images dripping with dread or blood have been a mainstay of Oliver Frey's illustrations, so it is no wonder that the genres of horror and extreme violent action gave him room to stretch his imagination.

FRIGHTENERS #1 cover
'Eric the Pie'
May 1991

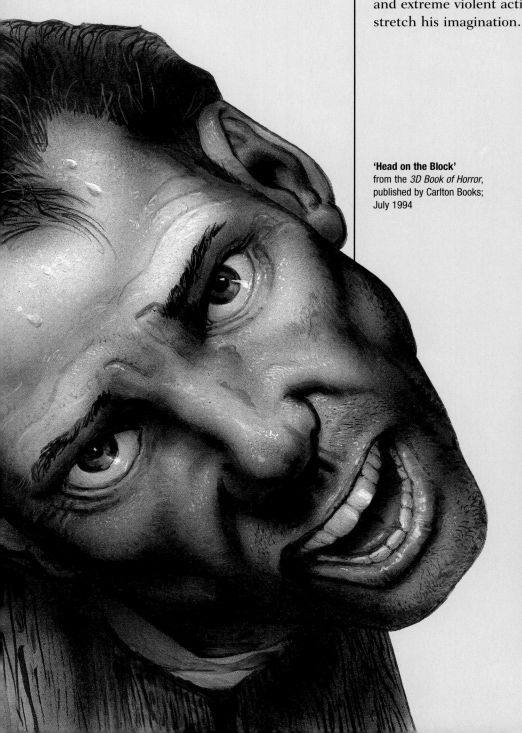

'Head on the Block'
from the *3D Book of Horror*,
published by Carlton Books;
July 1994

'Fear *magazine generally had a few short stories in each issue, and the feedback was so good to these that we decided to publish a magazine only containing shorts and novellas –* Frighteners. *We were fortunate enough to have attracted the attention of best-selling author Graham Masterton, who sent a manuscript called* Eric the Pie, *and this was my interpretation for the first* Frighteners. *I used my own National Health specs as the model for Eric's glasses – nice and nerdy. Unfortunately, some buyers at WH Smith, the main sellers for the new title, so objected to the cover that they pulled the magazine before it reached the shelves, and I had to replace Eric with something more anodyne.'*

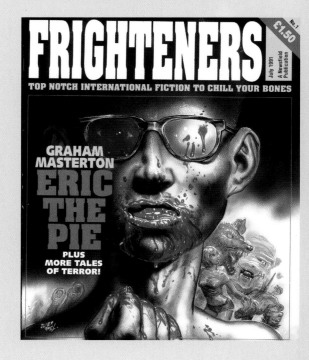

OLIVER
FREY
© NEWSFIELD PUBLICATIONS LTD 1986

ZZAP!64 #13 cover
'Cauldron II & Antiriad'
March 1986

'I enjoy doing horror pictures, it brings out the worst that lurks behind my rather timid façade…'

FEAR #6 cover
'Special Effects'
March 1989

'Which is the real face…?'

ZZAP!64 #35 poster
'Have a Heart – My
Valentine's Day'
January 1988

'I was inspired to do
this centrefold poster by
Gary Penn and Julian
Rignall, ZZAP!64's editor
and (at the time)
assistant, who definitely
did not want a cutesy
Valentine image.
Originally, the zombie
wore a ZZAP!64 logo on
his baseball cap, but I
later stuck the logo of a
new magazine called
Mega Machines over it,
and this was used as a
subscription
advertisement in
ZZAP!64 for pre-launch
publicity.'

AMTIX! #4 cover
'Way of the Tiger'
December 1985

Following pages:
ZZAP!64 #16 cover
'Green Beret'
June 1986

'From battle gore…'

ZZAP!64 #65 cover
'Murder'
July 1990

'– to classic whodunnit
designer splatter.'

FEAR #32 cover 'Vampires'
June 1991

'Dracula – always one of my "heroes".'

**CRASH #23 cover
'Friday The 13th'**
October 1985

'Many deemed this too sick for youngsters…'

CRASH #94 calendar
October 1991

'It's important that characters like these two always have far too many teeth to fit in the mouth…'

FEAR #8 cover
'Necroscope III'
June 1989

7 | HEROES AND VILLAINS

SEGA FORCE MEGA #V2.1
cover
'The Last Action Hero'
June 1993

OLIVER FREY.

War heroes, gladiators, sword and sorcery, kung-fu and barbarian warriors rapidly became staple fodder for computer games. Influenced in his informative years by cinema posters for big action movies such as the James Bond series and wartime thrillers like *The Guns of Navarone*, Oliver Frey was delighted to give reign to his passion for figures in action on magazine covers and posters. With an increased sophistication in both the graphics and gameplay, his range of 'heroes' was expanded to include many unlikely figures as well as the more obvious… and, of course, plenty of heinous villains.

COMMODORE FORCE #9
cover 'The Blues Brothers'
July 1993

133

SEGA FORCE MEGA #9 cover
'Mortal Kombat'
July 1993

AMTIX! #7 Cover
'Of Heroes and Monsters'
March 1986

Following pages:
CRASH #12 calendar
posters for 1985
October–November 1984

'An exercise in
ZX Spectrum
colour-branding…'

ZZAP!64 #20 cover
'Gauntlet'
October 1986

'The obvious fun here was making it seem as though the hero had thrust his way through a blank page leaving a hint of the "real" front cover behind him.'

CRASH #42 cover
'The Living Daylights–007'
May 1987

'This cover was almost destroyed by the quantity of other bits and pieces, including the announcement of a tie-in we had done with the irreverent Oink *comic.'* (See page 192)

CRASH #44 cover 'Renegade'
July 1987
(also reused for Amiga Force #5, May 1993)

**FEAR #14 cover 'Good Guy
Chucky from Child's Play'**
December 1989

CRASH #21 poster for 'Adventure Trail' column
August 1985

Later reused with suitable retitling as a poster in ZZAP!64 #7 (November 1985) for the Adventure Column as the 'White Wizard's Nightmare'.

**ZZAP!64 #52 cover
'Batman' and 'Astaroth –
Angel of Death'**
June 1989

*'Cover artwork was
often required to
combine two wholly
unrelated games and
still look good as a
single image…'*

**ZZAP!64 #46 cover
'Total Eclipse'**
December 1988

**Following pages:
ZZAP!64 #25 poster**
March 1987

and

**a generic 'war' calendar
poster for various titles**

*'This picture was
literally conceived of as
a "poster" for an
imaginary film, with
vignettes of mayhem
surrounding two central
heroic figures.'*

REALMS OF ARCANIA, Vol 1
1996

The California-based games book publishers Prima commissioned Frey to paint paperback covers for a trilogy of sword and sorcery novels based on the adventure game of the same name.

'I painted them with acrylics and inks, but then scanned them in and continued to "atmospherize" (as the American editor called it) them on computer.'

REALMS OF ARCANIA, Vol 2
1996

REALMS OF ARCANIA, Vol 3
1996

SEGA FORCE #15 cover
'Mick and Mack, Gladiators
for the World!'
January 1993

(Also used on the preview
edition of Sega Master Force
in June 1993)

'This Virgin Games
offering was a
McDonald's tie-in,
hence the baseball cap
logo. The artwork was
commissioned by Virgin
for the game cartridge's
inlay, but was never
used in the end.'

AMTIX! #2 cover 'Marsport'
October 1985

'This is one of my favourite paintings of the period – a classic science fiction adventure hero treading the keyboard of the computer that contains his world.'

CRASH #88 cover 'Wreckers'
March 1991

'I wanted this to look the stuff of 1950s pulp fiction magazines to fully do the slime justice.'

**ZZAP!64 #4 cover
'Beach Head II'**
June 1985

*'This originally featured
bursts of blood, but
when the software
house decided to use it
for the game packaging
I had to turn them into
"mud" to tone down the
violence.'*

**ZZAP!64 #34 cover
'Platoon'**
December 1987

*'I was pleased with the
effect of the pixellation,
which was achieved
with an airbrush and
not done on a
computer!'*

CRASH #11 cover
'Smashing Out of the
Spectrum'
October 1984

CRASH #92 cover
'Indiana Jones and the Fate
of Atlantis'
July 1991

CRASH Mail Order Advert
November 1983

'Once a week, as a young boy, I waited eagerly for the postman to arrive with my copy of Eagle. As far as I was concerned, the postman was a hero, so I went to town on this mail order advert. I imagined the thrill of the "Crash" mailman pulling up in his futuristic mail van, to hand me the latest Spectrum cassette – only, of course, my Postman Pat was a mechanoid.'

Scanned from the large-format transparency originally shot for repro in the first issue of *CRASH* – the original has been lost.

8 | WEIRD AND WONDERFUL

This section covers several pictures which do not fit into the regular staple of video game imagery, particularly covers for Newsfield's horror, science-fiction and fantasy periodical *Fear*. The highly influential magazine provided opportunities for Oliver Frey to create scenes of drama, often with a dynamic sense of composition to heighten the effect, as well as to work with some fine authors.

FEAR #27 interior art
'Satanist Orgy'
January 1991

SEGA FORCE #5 cover
'Lemmings'
March 1992

'The Lemmings *game had been out on several machines, always looking cute. I wanted something more frightening…'*

FEAR #27 cover
'Black Arts Special'
January 1991

'John Gilbert asked for something "dark, gloomy, erotic and fearful…" I think I gave him that. At the same time, I adapted the drawing into a line version for the Fear *T-shirt design.'*

FEAR #2 cover
Author James Herbert
July 1988

*'*Fear *editor John Gilbert couldn't wait to take the finished cover back to London with him and show it to James Herbert. He was said to be pleased with it…'*

Following pages:
FEAR #4 cover
'Something Wicked This Way Comes – Ray Bradbury'
November 1988

FEAR #1 cover
'Appetite for Horror'
May 1988

'The Bradbury cover is one of my favourites. His mix of the ordinary everyday with the gothic monstrous and weird, the loss of innocence and yet still with a sense of awe and wonder appealed. I wanted him to loom from space above Illinois-green grass, the grain silos and cattle, his imagination inspiring the youngster who stares in amazement at the marvellously fifties rocket ship. At the left lurks a hint of Bradbury terror.'

FRIGHTENERS #3 cover
'Guy N Smith's
The Executioner'
July 1991

CRASH #55
'Adventure Trail with
Samara'
June 1988

'Started as a doodle on the back of an envelope, this developed as it went along and now looks incredibly meaningful, when it is pure Egyptian-symbols hokum – maybe Dan Brown could unravel the riddle in his next "masterpiece"…'

FEAR #11 cover
'Haunting Halloween'
September 1989

CRASH #38 cover
'Wizard Wars"
January 1987

'This CRASH cover was typically a composite image featuring the month's two hit games, Feud and Ramarana. I lightly painted in the outline figures, then airbrushed blue and black over the whole, picking out the highlights with "bleed white".'

Following pages:
FEAR #9 cover
'Graham Masterton's
Dog Boys'
July 1989

'This Graham Masterton story was a strangely thrilling challenge to illustrate. An author can quite realistically suggest dogs with boys' heads, but translating what is accepted by the mind's eye onto flat board in a convincing visual is not easy. All I could do was warp and meld human with canine features, and aim for ensuing unpleasantness. I think it worked...'

FEAR #18 cover
'The Exorcist II'
April 1990

9 | A FREY MISCELLANY

Alexandra David-Néel
portrait for *Historical Atlas of Expeditions*, Checkmark Books (published 2000). Pencil and coloured crayons on paper; seen at original printed size.

David-Néel (1868–1969), a French explorer who trekked all over Central and East Asia, became the first European woman to enter Lhasa in Tibet.

'Crayons are not my normal medium, but I wanted to achieve a soft, romantic feel to the face, while at the same time portraying her tough determination.'

The Miscellany is devoted to work which falls outside the main scope of the stated aims of this book but serves to round out the appreciation of the sheer diversity of Frey's illustrating activity. The majority have been produced as illustrations for history books in a variety of techniques, ranging from traditional inks, acrylics and airbrush to electronic rendering, where the only 'original' exists as a line or halftone wash drawing, usually superseded by further work in Photoshop. All show his love of 'dramatic atmosphere'.

The large 'Snake Warrior' paintings on pages 184–5 have never before been published, and were done by Oliver for his own pleasure as part of a discontinued series. They were intended to be painted in oils, but the medium would not render the subtle gradations of colour he wanted, and a reversion to acrylics and airbrushed ink was inevitable.

'De Coronado's Trek'
Illustration in *Historical Atlas of Exploration*, Checkmark Books (published 1999). Ink wash and computer-rendered colour.

'Two examples (above and below) of how I make computer colour act like airbrushed ink with acrylic paint…'

'Battle in Sumer'
Illustration for *Living in Ancient Mesopotamia*, Facts On File – Checkmark Books (published 2006). Ink wash and digital colour.

'The Gunslinger'
Illustration for a feature in *Fear* magazine about Stephen King's 'Dark Tower' series. 1991, impasto acrylic on art board.

'The board is actually twice this height and width, since the text ran inside the illustration, but cropped, I feel the dynamic of the composition works.'

173

Coin and bust of Gaius Octavianus Julius Caesar Augustus, illustrations in *The Complete Chronicle of the Emperors of Rome*, Thalamus Publishing (published 2005).
Coin rendered in pencil, scanned and coloured on computer; bust in ink wash halftone, scanned and coloured on computer; original dimensions as seen.

LM MAGAZINE #2
December 1896

'It was something of a challenge to montage Holly Johnson (Frankie Goes to Hollywood), actor Paul McGann and get in a symbol of the Patrick McGoohan TV series The Prisoner, *with a touch of Port Meirion, where it was filmed.'*

'Rough Sea'
Lief Ericsson's voyage to Greenland for *Historical Atlas of the Viking World*, Checkmark Books (published 2002).
Pen and ink, with digital colour.

'Titanic'
Cover design for *The History of Shipwrecks*, Lyons Press (published 1999).
Line and halftone wash with digital colour.

'This was intended for the US edition of the book, but in the event a different image was used and this illustration featured much smaller on the interior pages. It was my second Titanic.

I painted the first more "traditionally" for a CRASH centrefold poster, which we later reused as a magazine cover. It was, of course, somewhat more dramatic in approach than the version I did for the "serious" shipwreck book.'

'Punk'
1985, ink and acryics on art board.

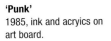

'Berserkirs'
Illustration in *Historical Atlas of the Viking World*, Checkmark Books (published 2002).
Pen and ink with computer-rendered colour.

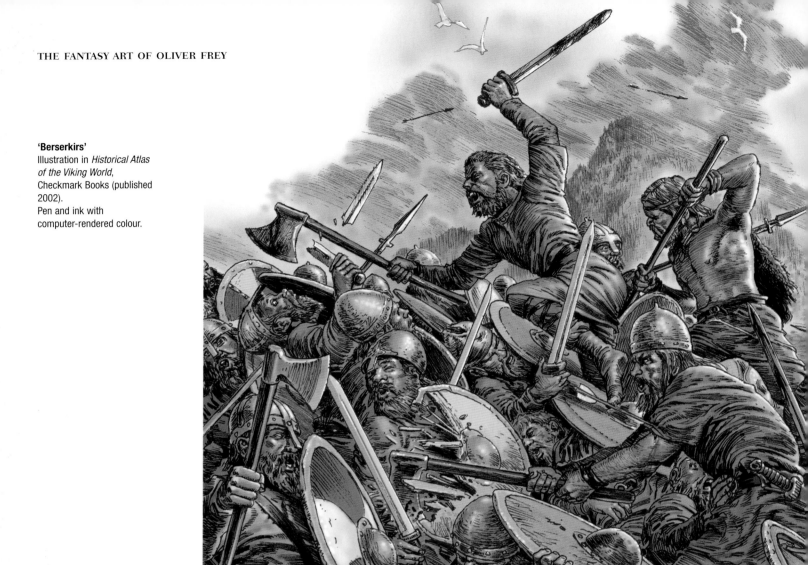

'Children's Crusade'
Illustration in *Historical Atlas of the Crusades*, Checkmark Books (published 2002). Pen, ink and wash on paper with digital colour.

'Death'
Illustration in *3D Horror*, published by Carlton Books (1996).

'Druid Sacrifice'
Chapter opener illustration in
Historical Atlas of the Celtic World, Checkmark Books
(published 2001).
Pen and ink with
digital colour.

Following page:
'Stanley in Africa'
Title page illustration for
Historical Atlas of Expeditions,
Checkmark Books (published
2000). Ink halftone wash with
digital colour.

Far left: Snake Warriors 1
1996. Acrylic and airbrushed
ink on hardboard;
105 x 69 cm; 41 x 27 in

Left: Snake Warriors 2
1997. Acrylic and airbrushed
ink on hardboard;
42 x 110 cm; 16.5 x 43 in

Left below: Illustration of the
use of Greek Fire in the book
*Forgotten Power – Byzantium
– Bulwark of Christianity*
Thalamus Publishing
(published 2006).
August 2005
Ink halftone and
digital colour.

Illustration for an article on
Levi's 501s, *Attitude*
magazine, May 2005
Ink and wash on paper.

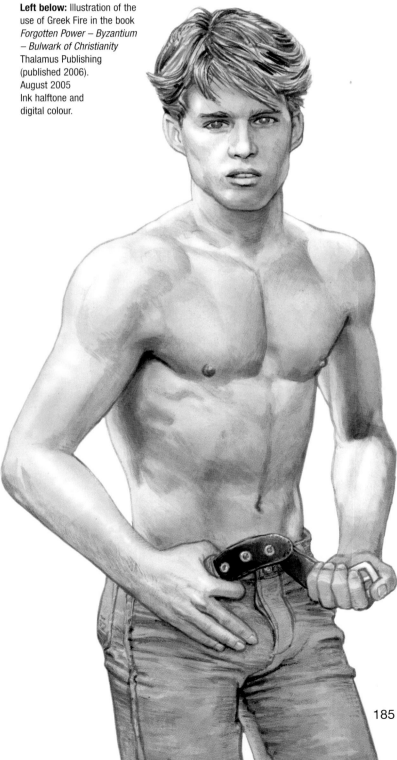

ART TECHNIQUES

In the late 1980s Newsfield was at the forefront of electronic publishing, so it was inevitable that at some point Oliver Frey would discard the paint brush and airbrush for digital art; but not without initial reservations. Most of his work for the Newsfield magazines was painted using an airbrush to create large areas of background colour, with details added using pen or brush. 'I like the airbrush because it is simple,' he said at the time, 'and it is a very quick method of applying colour and adding effects. It's a time-saver. I remember one painting I did for *Look & Learn*, in which the foremast of a ship is shrouded in mist (*pages 22–23*). All I had to do was paint the mast and rigging in solid black and then airbrush colour over it to give the effect of mist. If I had attempted that using ordinary brushes it could have taken days to achieve the effect, rather than a couple of hours.'

In the mid-1980s, Oliver had been using an airbrush for only five or six years. Most of his comic work was created using traditional brush and pen techniques, using inks and acrylics. 'It's easy to overpaint with acrylics, but you have to be more careful in the planning stage when you're using inks and an airbrush, especially in masking off areas to be left white. Generally, I'll produce a pencil rough onto the board, and then spray the background and large areas of colour on top, adding the fine detail by hand.'

The airbrush became a distinctive mark of an Oliver Frey illustration, although he never really came to love the instrument. 'I'm not very good at coping with technical things, and equipment,' he once confessed. How about the computer then? In a 1985 interview, he firmly denied he would use one for artwork. 'I've never been tempted to get involved with computer art – I'm not really very patient. I find it difficult enough coping with the airbrush and I couldn't sit down in front of a computer and fiddle endlessly with the mouse and keyboard to produce the result that I wanted.'

Famous last words

But in 1990, Oliver did begin to experiment with the Apple Macintosh to produce illustrations. 'Enthusiasts tried me out on an electronic drawing pad, but I couldn't get on with it. It simply isn't how I draw, and the early ones were so slow and clumsy, I've never bothered again.' He used Adobe Illustrator for a while, but it also failed the Frey drawing test: 'Far too object-oriented (horrible "vectors" and bezier curves), technical and cold.'

However, Adobe's other major art tool proved to be a different matter. Thanks to Newsfield's technical journal for the developing electronic publishing market called *PrePress*, beta copies of new software arrived for testing, including a colour separation program called Photoshop. 'It was fantastic, even though those early versions were primitive compared to today's,' Oliver recalls.

Over two to three years, he gradually moved away from inks and the

Creating a Roman coin of Majorian for *The Complete Chronicle of the Emperors of Rome* (Thalamus Publishing, 2005)

Stage 1: Pencil drawing of traced version of coin photo scanned in line; converted to colour and the layer set to 'multiply'.

Stage 2: Underpainting layer coloured with various Photoshop brushes from a strict colour palette.

Stage 3: Offset drop shadow layer made by copying the colour layer, preserving transparency and filling, before using gaussian blur.

Stage 4: The finished coin.

airbrush until, in recent years, he has produced almost all his work on the computer. 'In a way, it's a shame – all you end up with is a digital file, there's no physical board with colour and texture on it, nothing to frame and hang on the wall. When you paint by hand, the acrylics or the ink are never quite perfectly laid down on the paper or board. There are always tiny artefacts caused by the hand. In Photoshop, everything is perfect, and because you can zoom in so close, you tend to become obsessed with pixel-perfect alignment.'

To a degree, he gets around this problem through something that has not changed since the earliest days – drawing. 'I begin with a used envelope and a biro and sketch out incredibly rough ideas as thumb-nails. What is mostly seen is a swirl of lines indicating composition and motion. No one understands them, but I can interpret them later with a pencil on paper at full size. For a "line-and-wash" illustration I scan the pencil drawing in bitmap line [at 300dpi].

'In Photoshop I convert the bitmap to greyscale, then colour [CMYK for print books]. The scan is still in a line form so it's easy to grab and delete out the white background to transparent. After that I can colour the line any way I want, and start adding the colour detail in layers underneath. Sometimes, just naturally, the painting under- or overlaps the line, forming those artefacts of the hand-painted version. It's very small, but it adds that touch of life to the finished work.

'In the case of a halftone, I paint over the pencil drawing with black ink, from hard line to the faintest wash, scan it as a greyscale halftone and convert to colour. The drawing layer is then set to either "darken" or "multiply", possibly re-coloured itself, before brushing other colours and effects on separate layers.'

Oliver's refusal to abandon the old-fashioned discipline of drawing sets his illustrations apart from much other computer-generated art, giving them the feeling of a lively surface texture that, in reality, is not there. The airbrush and compressor have remained in the attic. 'There's no way around it, a Photoshop airbrush doesn't smell like vomit – the special inks smelled as though someone had thrown up – it never clogs up, you don't have to wash everything to change colours, and you never get dirty fingernails.'

The stages in a 'line-and-wash' illustration of the Babylonian king Hammurabi and his astrologer for a forthcoming children's series on daily life in ancient times. **Left:** Extremely rough sketches in biro on the back of an envelope develop the composition. **Below, top to bottom:** The scanned line layer, multiplied, is recoloured to suit; the underpainting layer rendered with Photoshop brushes; the combined layers in the finished panel.

Another aspect of his work that has not changed much with the computer is a handy mirror. Oliver suffers the common complaint of astigmatism, an eye condition in which imperfections in the curvature of the eyeball tend to distort the vision. 'Particularly, my faces look a bit lopsided. Holding up the drawing to a mirror makes the distortion obvious, so I can compensate. On the other hand, few faces are really symmetrical, so between original distortion and subsequent compensation, I think my people have a human touch sometimes lacking in the work of others.' Oliver is left-handed, and yet on the computer it is his right hand that does all the intricate mouse work. 'When I first began using a computer, it usually belonged to another member of staff and was inevitably set up right-handed. So I just picked up the mouse in that hand and started "painting".'

Nearly all of Oliver's pictures are set in the past or the future – including the pure fantasy illustrations. The games magazines of the 1980s and early 90s provided him with both in abundance, or at least fantasy adventure such as James Bond. Today, he spends more time with historical subjects in reference books.

'I've never really liked the Here And Now – the Now doesn't really inspire me. All my paintings are bigger than life, mainly because life isn't as exciting as it can appear in pictures. I escape into the picture I'm painting. When I'm really concentrating I imagine I'm really there, looking onto the action in the painting – otherwise it's difficult to see the things in my mind's eye. It can take a couple of hours for me to go away from a picture – when I finish I sometimes spend an hour just sitting and staring at it. I'm in an alternate reality, I suppose. To work, the picture has to be convincing to me, which means I have to get really involved in what's happening.' Which accounts for some of the rather strange facial expressions that sometimes rest on Oli's face when he's drawing a monster or an action sequence.

'I've always been a romantic dreamer. Ever since the games I played as a child, I've been able to get totally immersed in a fantasy world. I suppose it must say something about my psyche that I was always the baddie, never the Brave Sheriff, always the evil (naturally doomed) SS monster, never the War Hero. Other than fantasy I'm passionate about history. History may be about real people but, lacking photographs, their lives and actions have to be imagined in a believable way. I enjoy illustrating historical scenes, even though it involves quite a lot of reference work for accuracy. In some ways it's simpler to draw futuristic scenes and fantasy – the referencing isn't a problem because I make it all up, and it's just a matter of producing a painting that has its own accuracy and detail.

'What I'd really like to do is direct a film. Film is the ultimate fantasy-fulfilling medium. The closest you can get to film in a printed way is a comic strip, and there are a lot of common elements. I'd still like to be the director, sitting above a massive battle sequence with thousands of extras all re-enacting a scene from history. I would really be there, in control of the ultimate fantasy....'

At the time of completing this book, this illustration of priests observing the rise of the new moon from a ziggurat in Babylon shown on this page represented the most recent of Frey's pieces of digital working.

'It took a while to develop the original "envelope" sketch to an ink painting on paper in order to get the perspective and sense of height correct. The top image on the left shows a part of the original painting after scanning in greyscale, which was set to "multiply".

'The middle image shows the underpainting layer, done with blends, airbrush and brushes. I use various levels of opacity and often set brushes to "darken" or "lighten", depending on the effect I want to get.

'The bottom image is an overpainting layer to carry the more finished detail and highlights, such as the moon, twilight on building edges and smoke. Of course, it is a transparent layer, but I superimposed it on black here for the sake of clarity.'

INDEX OF COVERS

Magazine covers were the most prominent of Oliver Frey's artwork during the 1980s and early 90s. For reference purposes, this index shows the artwork, combined with the magazine cover elements, in the order in which they appear in the book (page numbers in bold) excepting those already appearing on pages beside the original. Dates given here are the month of publication. In general terms, the painting would have been produced approximately two months prior to the month given for publication.

41 CRASH #15
April 1985

42 CRASH #2
March 1984

43 ZZAP!64 #2
June 1985

44 CRASH #20
September 1985

46 ZZAP!64 #18 October 1986

47 AMTIX! #9
July 1986

48 ZZAP!64 #10
February 1986

49 ZZAP!64 #77
September 1991

52 ZZAP!64 #6
October 1985

53 CRASH #9
October 1984

54 CRASH #24 December 1985

55 CRASH #35
December 1986

58 CRASH #5
June 1984

59 CRASH #21
October 1985

60 ZZAP!64 #30
October 1987

61 CRASH #98
April 1992

64 AMTIX 'Issue Zero'
October 1985

64 AMTIX! #1
November 1985

65 CRASH #16
May 1985

66 ZZAP!64 #31
November 1987

67 ZZAP!64 #42
October 1988

74 ZZAP!64 #7
November 1985

75 CRASH #87
April 1991

78 SEGA FORCE MEGA
#V2.3 October 1993

79 CRASH #80
September 1990

80 ZZAP!64 #76
August 1991

81 CRASH #51
April 1988

82 AMIGA FORCE #11
November 1993

83 CRASH #49
February 1988

84 ZZAP!64 #8
December 1985

85 ZZAP!64 #68
December 1990

92 CRASH #4
May 1984

93 CRASH #25
February 1986

94–5 ZZAP!64 #12
April 1986

96 ZZAP!64 #9
January 1986

97 AMTIX! #1
January 1987

98 CRASH #13
February 1985

99 ZZAP!64 #23
March 1987

100 SEGA FORCE #4
April 1992

109 CRASH #8
September 1984

110 ZZAP!64 #15
July 1986

111 ZZAP!64 #29
September 1987

112 ZZAP!64 #71 March 1991

113 CRASH #19
August 1985

114 ZZAP!64 #39
July 1988

116 CRASH #79
August 1990

117 ZZAP!64 #87
August 1992

119 ZZAP!64 #50
June 1989

122 ZZAP!64 #13
May 1986

123 FEAR #6
May 1989

125 AMTIX! #4
February 1986

126 ZZAP!64 #16
August 1986

127 ZZAP!64 #65
September 1990

128 FEAR #32
August 1991

191

129 CRASH #23
December 1985

131 FEAR #8
August 1989

133 COMMODORE FORCE #9
September 1993

134 SEGA FORCE MEGA #9
September 1993

135 AMTIX! #7
May 1986

138 ZZAP!64 #20
December 1996

139 CRASH #42
July 1987

140 CRASH #44
September 1987

141 FEAR #14
February 1990

144 ZZAP!64 #52
August 1989

145 ZZAP!64 #46
February 1989

151 SEGA FORCE #15
March 1993

152 AMTIX! #2 December
1985

153 CRASH #88
May 1991

154 ZZAP!64 #4
August 1985

155 ZZAP!64 #34
February 1988

156 CRASH #11
December 1984

157 CRASH #92
September 1991

161 SEGA FORCE #5
May 1992

162 FEAR #2
September 1988

163 FEAR #27
March 1991

164 FEAR #4
January 1989

165 FEAR #1
July 1988

166 FRIGHTENERS #3
September 1991

169 FEAR #11
November 1989

168 CRASH #38
March 1987

170 FEAR #9
September 1989

171 FEAR #18
June 1990

175 LM MAGAZINE #2
February 1987